The Blueprint for Aspiring and New Teachers

The Blueprint for Aspiring and New Teachers

The Habits of a Winner

Alexandria J. Chyrack

To all who have ever dreamed of being a teacher. Do not give up on the dream!

Although the author and publisher have made every effort to ensure that the information in this book was correct at the time of first publication, the author and publisher do not assume and hereby disclaim any liability to any party for any loss, damage, or disruption caused by errors or omissions, whether such errors or omissions result from negligence, accident, or any other cause.

Copyright © 2025 by Alexandria J. Chyrack

All rights reserved. No part of this book may be reproduced or transmitted in any form or by any means, electronic or mechanical, including photocopying, recording, or any information storage and retrieval system, without permission in writing from the author.

ISBN: 978-1-6653-1030-7 - Paperback
eISBN: 978-1-6653-1031-4 - eBook

These ISBNs are the property of BookLogix for the express purpose of sales and distribution of this title. The content of this book is the property of the copyright holder only. BookLogix does not hold any ownership of the content of this book and is not liable in any way for the materials contained within. The views and opinions expressed in this book are the property of the Author/Copyright holder, and do not necessarily reflect those of BookLogix.

Library of Congress Control Number: 2025908893

⊚This paper meets the requirements of ANSI/NISO Z39.48-1992 (Permanence of Paper)

0 7 1 4 2 5

"And we know that in all things God works for the good of those who love him, who have been called according to his purpose."

—Romans 8:28 (NIV)

I decided to write this guide because one was not given to me. God put this idea in my heart and my hope is it will encourage you to chase excellence.

What is your plan for today, tomorrow, next week, next month, and next year? My son plays football and there is always a game plan. Create your plan now. What are your goals and visions?

One

WAKE UP EARLY.

I wake up at 5 a.m. This gives me time for myself when I can read my Bible and pray to the Lord. I also make my breakfast and lunch. Set a timer so you know when it is time to leave and give yourself extra time in case there is traffic. This is very important during your commute. Make sure you use your time wisely. You can listen to your favorite motivational speaker, learn a new language, or listen to uplifting music. Listening to something positive while you are driving to work will help you feel encouraged. Do the same for your commute home.

Two

THINK ABOUT THE TYPE OF TEACHER YOU WANT TO BE REMEMBERED AS.

What are you doing to inspire your students and coworkers? Will your students remember your name for a good reason? Take some time to think about this.

Three

BREAKFAST IS VERY IMPORTANT.

You want a nutritious meal that will sustain you throughout your day. As a teacher, you will be on your feet, and you want to make sure you have enough energy to do so.

Four

PACK A LUNCH.

I pack my lunch daily because I want to know what I will be eating. You may not be happy with the meal the cafeteria has that day. Packing your own lunch will eliminate any disappointment and save you a substantial amount of money if lunch is not included for teachers. I have saved over $700 yearly. You can take the money you save and put it into savings, invest it, buy books, or use it for a vacation.

Five

LOOK AT YOURSELF IN THE MIRROR AND KNOW YOU ARE IMPORTANT!

You have been *chosen to teach.* Do not take this lightly. Your students are depending on you. Put on an attitude for success. You are a winner, and this is a new day, and it will never be here again. Make it count!

Six

DRESS THE PART.

If you aspire to be a teacher, look at how teachers dress. Do not think you do not have the money to do that yet. There are numerous stores where you can find great outfits! Start purchasing clothing you will enjoy wearing when you become a teacher. If you are already a teacher, get creative with your outfits. My students always compliment me on my clothing. They notice everything! Oh, and you will want to wear comfortable shoes. You should invest in good-quality shoes that will keep your feet feeling amazing throughout your day!

Seven

KEEP TRACK OF TIME.

Invest in a watch. I have a smart watch and it helps me throughout the day. One day my niece complimented me on my punctuality. I thought it was so cute! She said she wanted to get better at being on time. I told her the first thing you need to do is say you are good at being on time. I asked her where her watch was, and she said she did not have one. I made sure she got one that same day!

Eight

ENCOURAGE YOURSELF.

Years ago, while I was in Harlem, New York, I saw Muhammad Ali! I gave him a hug. I was so excited because he was one of the greatest boxers ever. If you have seen clips of Muhammad Ali in the past, he was always encouraging himself. Sometimes we will not have anyone around encouraging us. Not our supervisor, colleagues, students, family, and friends. Just remember, do not quit! You will not always be encouraged by the people around you. You must be your biggest fan and make sure to learn from your mistakes. People are not consistent, but our God is and he loves you. Remember to chase excellence in and outside the classroom, and know you are valuable. Even if others may not notice, you are valuable!

Nine

EXERCISE.

You want to incorporate some form of exercise daily. This is important for your health. I try to include at least thirty minutes per day of exercise. Walking is a great way to get your body moving, and it does not cost you a thing! Use your watch to help you. I find that my smart watch is very helpful with keeping track of my exercise goals.

Ten

ARRIVE AT SCHOOL EARLIER THAN YOU NEED TO.

If you have an electric vehicle, make sure it is charged and ready to go. If your car takes gasoline, make sure to get it the day before. Also, sometimes gas station pumps are closed—looking for gas would not be a good way to start your morning. Do not be there too early, and not right on time. I would say at least twenty minutes earlier than you need to be there. This will give you time to make copies, check your mail and email, and get your classroom organized.

Eleven

READ.

Try to read for at least thirty minutes a day. This is a great way to continue learning. I enjoy reading all different types of books, especially ones where I learn something new!

Twelve

DO NOT SPEND TOO MUCH TIME ON SOCIAL MEDIA.

Use your watch and set an alarm for twenty minutes or less daily. Once the alarm goes off, you need to move on and do something else.

Thirteen

ALWAYS HAVE SUPPLIES FOR YOUR STUDENTS, ESPECIALLY PENCILS.

You will notice some students do not have notebooks, pencils, folders, and other items. Do not ignore this. Make sure you discreetly ask the student about their supplies. The student may have forgotten them at home or may not have any. Always have extra so you can give a student a notebook, folder, or whatever they need. I teach social studies, and I give all my students a folder at the beginning of the school year because this helps them to stay organized. Some of my students may lose their folder, and that is all right. I just give them another one.

Fourteen

DECORATE YOUR CLASSROOM.

Your classroom should reflect yourself and what you want the students to know about. Take your time decorating your classroom. You may even want to think of a theme for the year. One year, my theme was football, and I put up motivational quotes from Vince Lombardi. Make it your own and take care and pride in your decorating. If you feel you need assistance, ask one of your coworkers. They may give you some great ideas.

Fifteen

KEEP YOUR CLASSROOM ORGANIZED.

This will save you time because you will know where everything is throughout the day.

Sixteen

HAVE A WINNING ATTITUDE.

During your day, you may feel defeated. Do not let it show. Have the attitude of a winner. Your coworkers and students will appreciate this attitude, and it will spread! Again, be a winner!

Seventeen

KNOW YOUR STUDENTS' NAMES.

This is important because each student is unique and special, and they want to feel that way. Make a point of learning all your students' names and the correct pronunciation. I had to learn over one hundred and ten names one year, and I did it. At the beginning of the school year, I would ask the students to please give me grace, and they did.

Eighteen

GET INVOLVED.

We are all busy, but we should give back and serve others. This can be in the form of becoming a sponsor for a club. Remember, your school needs you!

Nineteen

LOYALTY TO YOUR TEAM.

There will be parent conferences, meetings, and other things you will need to attend. Your team is depending on you to be trustworthy and dependable. Make sure you are a part of a strong team.

Twenty

BECOME A GOOD LISTENER.

Do not speak over anyone. Sometimes your coworkers and students need someone to speak to. Always be present in the conversation and do not interrupt them. Maintain eye contact with them and show genuine interest in what they are telling you.

Twenty-One

SHOW EMPATHY WHEN YOU CAN.

You never know what someone is going through.

Twenty-Two

GIVE GRACE, PLEASE!

If a student leaves an assignment or something to that effect, please allow them time to complete it. Especially if the student normally turns in their assignments on time. We are not perfect, and if we were to forget something, we would want someone to give us grace. Do not be too rigid.

Twenty-Three

HAVE AN AGENDA.

I have an agenda on my board every day. This helps keep me on track for my lesson, and it tells the students what we are going to do for the day. I have had coworkers compliment me on keeping an agenda on the board. This is especially helpful if you are being observed in your classroom. The administrator, professor, or other individual can follow along.

Twenty-Four

KEEP UP WITH DEADLINES.

A portable calendar is a great place to keep all your upcoming priorities.

Twenty-Five

BRAINSTORM WITH YOUR COLLEAGUES TO COME UP WITH THE BEST LESSON PLANS.

Plan your lessons in advance; you can always make changes to alter or improve them during the day.

Twenty-Six

HAVE A MENTOR.

This is very important. If one is not assigned to you, find one! Your mentor does not have to be in your school. They should be someone you admire and can gain wisdom from, preferably in your same subject. I have a mentor, and it is great having someone to gain knowledge from. Not only do I have a mentor, but I have some great colleagues who have helped me out tremendously, and I am truly thankful. One day, you may be asked to be a mentor, so gain as much insight as you can so you can share it with your future mentee.

Twenty-Seven

DRINK WATER.

During the day, you want to stay hydrated. Fill your water bottle at home. This will save you time and money looking for a vending machine. Also, you do not want to complain about the taste of the water from the water fountain. Bringing your own will help you avoid this.

Twenty-Eight

IF YOU WEAR GLASSES, BRING THEM WITH YOU.

Make sure to have two pairs just in case you misplace one. You do not want to get to work and not be able to read because you left your glasses at home.

Twenty-Nine

ALWAYS EXPECT THE UNEXPECTED.

I must say, I can have a lesson planned and know how my day is going to go. Then a student may get sick, or a fight may break out. Be ready for everything *now*. Always know where the exits are and report anything suspicious to your supervisor. Also, if you have emergency buttons in your classroom, make sure they work.

Thirty

SECURE YOUR VALUABLES.

Unfortunately, we live in a society where sometimes people want to take something that is not theirs. Always keep anything of value locked away. Tell your students to keep up with their belongings and let them know you have students who come in and out of your classroom, and it is their responsibility to keep their items with them.

Thirty-One

ALWAYS KEEP YOUR KEYS WITH YOU.

If you do not have a lanyard, I suggest purchasing one. They are very affordable and will save you from looking for your keys or locking yourself out of your classroom.

Thirty-Two
TAKE RESTROOM BREAKS.

If you need to use the restroom, make sure to notify a coworker or your supervisor. Do not leave your classroom unattended. If a student needs to use the restroom, let them. Speak with your supervisor about the restroom policy when it is not a scheduled restroom break. You do not want the student to have an accident, so make sure you know what your plan is beforehand.

Thirty-Three

KEEP YOUR CELLPHONE ON VIBRATE AND TRY NOT TO HAVE IT OUT TOO MUCH DURING THE SCHOOL DAY.

If your watch is capable of receiving messages and emails, do that instead. You do not want to be the teacher who tells students to put their cell phones away but is on their cell phone while teaching the lesson. I know emergencies happen when you cannot avoid being on the phone but try your best to put the cell phone down.

Thirty-Four

USE KIND WORDS.

When I was in middle school and high school, I did not have one teacher say a positive word to me. I had a teacher in high school tell me I needed to get a life. I do not remember his name, but I do remember what he said and how he made me feel. It was not until I attended college that I saw how an educator could really develop their students. I will never forget my history teacher, Dr. White. I remember his name because he was a difference maker. He took his role seriously and encouraged students to ask questions. He would listen to us and make us feel seen and valued. After I graduated, I asked him to write a letter of recommendation for me. He took so long I thought he forgot about it! I contacted him and he said he was working on it. I finally received the letter and was blown away by the level of detail. It was over two pages long! I had never received a letter of recommendation like that before. I still have the letter, and it helped me get hired as a teacher. My students ask me all the time to write letters of recommendation for them. I always tell them be careful how you treat people, because you never know when you may need a letter of recommendation. If you have not written a letter of recommendation for a student before, think of it as a great opportunity. Always encourage your students and have something positive to say.

Thirty-Five

KEEP YOUR CLASSROOM A SAFE SPACE FOR EVERYONE.

If you hear any unkind words or talk of violence, do not ignore this. You may discreetly address the student saying the threats and contact a counselor or an administrator if you think a student may be getting bullied. Do not leave this for someone else to take care of. You do not want something to happen to the student if it could have been prevented.

Thirty-Six

ALWAYS HAVE YOUR CLASS ROSTER DURING FIRE DRILLS AND FIELD TRIPS.

Keep a head count.

Thirty-Seven

BE AWARE OF STUDENT ALLERGIES AND FIRST AID.

In case of an emergency, it is important to know what may trigger an allergic reaction. Some of your students may need an inhaler for asthma and some may use an autoinjector. If your school does not offer CPR/AED classes, I suggest you invest in a class that will provide this information. Additionally, washing your hands throughout the day and utilizing hand sanitizer can help prevent the spread of germs and mitigate sickness. This also applies to students! The students will benefit from having access to supplies such as hand sanitizer and tissues.

Thirty-Eight

MAINTAIN THE CLEANLINESS OF YOUR CLASSROOM.

You never know who may enter, so you want to be prepared.

Thirty-Nine

GIVE REWARDS.

I love getting a reward, and so do your students. Set up a reward system that can help the students stay on task and feel proud of completing assignments.

Forty

STAY IN TOUCH WITH PARENTS.

It is crucial that you have communication with your students' parents. You will need to know if a student is sick or if there is something happening in the home. Keep communication open.

Forty-One

COMMUNICATION IS KEY!

If you know you are going to be out of the office, make sure your supervisor and team members are aware of your upcoming absence. Do not leave the school building without informing a supervisor. You do not want your supervisor or coworkers to wonder where you are. Even in the case of student-teaching, a lack of clear communication could negatively reflect on you and your school. Try your best to schedule your absence/absences in advance. Speak with your team and keep them informed.

Forty-Two

ALLOW YOUR STUDENTS TO USE THEIR CREATIVITY.

I have a gifted endorsement, and I let my students think out of the box instead of putting them in a box. They are constantly surprising me with their creativity. When you can, be flexible and allow students to use their creativity. You will be amazed at their numerous gifts and talents.

Forty-Three

DON'T EVER STOP LEARNING.

It is important that you continue to gain knowledge. Classrooms are changing, and so is the use of technology. Stay up to date and incorporate technology into your classroom. Attend seminars and classes that will help strengthen you as a teacher.

<u>Forty-Four</u>

MOVE SEATS IF YOU NEED TO.

During the school year, I do have to move some of my students' seats. This may be because of too much talking, or they may be off task constantly. I have noticed when I move a student's seat closer to me, the student is able to stay on task and focus. Here is an example of this. I had a student who was on the verge of failing my social studies class. We had a parent-teacher conference regarding the student's academic performance. I moved the student's seat closer to my desk, and I noticed the student started to focus more. The student was able to get their grade up and passed the class. I said to the student, "You must be so proud." The student smiled and was happy. Remember to constantly encourage your students throughout the school year.

Forty-Five

ALWAYS SHOW RESPECT TOWARDS EVERYONE IN THE SCHOOL.

It does not matter what their position is. Treat people how you want to be treated.

Forty-Six

SHOW INTEGRITY.

You want to be a teacher who keeps their word. You should always strive to do your best in all situations.

Forty-Seven

WEAR A SMILE WHEN YOU CAN!

This may be difficult for some, but your coworkers and students will appreciate seeing you smile. I know this because I try it, and you know what? The students sometimes smile back at me.

Forty-Eight

GET IT DONE TODAY!

Do not ever put off doing what you can do today by doing it tomorrow.

Forty-Nine

HAVE A CURRENT PASSPORT.

I had the opportunity to travel to Oaxaca, Mexico, with my daughter in 2024. I enjoyed the experience and the people we encountered really showed hospitality. I believe wherever you are, you should serve others. This is what I did in Oaxaca, Mexico. I became a sponsor with an organization that works with children who need assistance. Let your light shine in and out of the classroom.

Fifty

DO NOT GIVE UP!

I was a teacher assistant for five years before I was hired as a teacher. Those five years gave me the experience I needed, and nothing is ever wasted. I remember when I would be making copies or cleaning the students' desks and thinking to myself, *I cannot wait to have my own classroom one day.* When I interviewed for a seventh-grade gifted social studies teacher position, the principal mentioned that I had a lot of experience. I was thrilled when I was offered the position!

1. **Take care of yourself.** Schedule your annual physicals, dentist appointments, and all other appointments. Remember you

are a leader, and you should strive to be happy and healthy in the classroom.

2. **Have a financial strategy.** Find out if your job comes with a pension, 403 (b), and life insurance. There should be a human resources department that can give you more details. Make sure you set up beneficiaries for all your accounts.

   My employer offers free will preparation. I took advantage of this and met with an attorney and had my will prepared all for free. You should also set up an account where you are saving a percentage of your earnings in case of an emergency. You may want to speak with a financial advisor on the best plan of action for you. I did, and it really helped me plan for my future. I was delighted to learn that I was on my way to becoming a millionaire. Also, find out what your retirement plan is. Are you vested after a certain number of years? These are questions you need to know. Find this information out sooner rather than later.

3. **Always demonstrate courage, strength, and perseverance.** When I was in college, I received the Gloria Waldman Award for Courage, Strength, and Perseverance. I hope everyone who reads this guide will continue to strive for all three and be successful in and outside of the classroom.

About the Author

Alexandria J. Chyrack was born and raised in Harlem, New York, and currently lives in Georgia with her family. Alexandria has received an associate's degree in paralegal studies, a bachelor of arts in history, a master of arts in educational studies, gifted endorsement, and a certification in biblical studies.

Not only is Alexandria a social studies teacher, she is also an author, public speaker, business owner, paralegal, notary, and a member of Sigma Gamma Rho Sorority, Inc.

www.ingramcontent.com/pod-product-compliance
Lightning Source LLC
Chambersburg PA
CBHW072137070526
44585CB00016B/1714